THE LIGHTHOUSE

HEALING AND HOME

CHARU MONI

Dedication

To my Ane,

For making me believe that if it isn't a crazy idea, it isn't a dream.

With loads of love,

Your Tuna

Contents

Contents

Contents

Preface

"*Dear Diary,*

Today Yam Saro Maam appreciated me for the way I wrote my answers. She called out many names in the class and appreciated us all, but the first one she called out was my name. I am very happy today because she appreciated me for my writings. She also said that I can be a great poet someday and that I should dream big and strong. Well, coming back to tell you about the day, we were asked to write about the things that we often wonder and I wrote that I am just vey curious about how poets pen down so many beautiful verses and what actually goes inside their mind and that it must be as big as the universe I guess.

I know that it is just a small gesture, but I just feel so happy when someone says that they like the way I write, and that they can relate to whatever things I pen down. Just imagine, me, being a writer someday and having a book of my own and people reading it, it would be such a joy. I think then, I would be the happiest girl in the whole wide world. I know that I am thinking about days far too ahead, but you never know, what tomorrow brings and I am very hopeful for the days to come.

> *P.S : I have classes tomorrow and I have to take my leave. Bye!*
> *Love,*
> *Moni.* "

This is an abstract from a diary entry of mine from 2012, when I was in class seven. I liked how the young Moni was so hopeful for the days to come and all the good things she used to dream about. So, this is like a gift that I want to give to the younger version of myself for believing in me and encouraging me to hold onto my dreams. By reading the old notes I wrote to myself, I felt that my words would mean nothing if they die without being known to the world and that all the things that once meant so much to me would end up into nothing if I let it die inside my head.

"The Lighthouse" is a collection of the verses I wrote for the people and for myself. It represents the love that people showered over me and all the things that occured in the way of life. It is the tale of the miseries, love, healing and recovery.

With this, I bring to you my debut book that has the greatest role to play in my life. I hope you like what I wrote with my whole heart and soul.

Thank You.

Acknowledgements

This Anthology seemed like a distant dream a few years ago and I cannot be happier that that dream is today, a reality. I am thankful to all the souls I met on my way of this poetic journey. People that inspired, people that believed ,people that had kept their faith on me, people that has stood the test of all the bad times and people that stood firm like "A Lighthouse" when the storm in me arosed and I did not have any idea on what to do and how to move on in life again.

Starting from the roots, I would like to thank two most important people in my life other than my own very family without whom this dream would've still be living in the shadows of the dark pages of my diary. My Vikash Rai Sir, who I lost touch with but who was the first person in my life to ever inspire me to pen my thoughts. Thank you Sir for being such a great friend and the best teacher too.And I like to thank my Mentor, My Counselor and a person I look upto, My Monroe Maam. A person who helped me put this scattered paper of writings into something so original of mine. Thank you Maam for existing and for being such a good friend and a teacher at the same time.

I am happy to tell my JNV Family that the dream we once dreamt together is now a reality and the credit runs to all of you, each one of you. Because without the readers to read my poems in the tender days of my rebellious period, I would not have had the faith in me to move on with the journey I took upon myself.

It is possible because of you all. My Mom and Dad for having the greatest faith in me .My Sister, Nani, for being a critic and a voice that always points out the bitter and sweet in me. My Entire family for supporting me. My Kai Larku for telling me that you'll support me no matter what I end up with.

I would also like to thank Notion Press for giving wings to my dream and making it posibble for me. Thank you for your greatest support and effort for making my life long dream, a reality.

A shoutout and deepest gratitude to the most favourite people of mine in this world entire world my friends, Aku, Boni, Feena, Omi, Yashni (My MOBFAY), Ame, Adum, Anya, Ana, Asha, Achup, My entire team of Aravali. Venilu, Mayi, Elimi, Gitika, Mito, Omin, Ana, Achup,Puja, Kiran,Linda, Etu, Swastikha, Tadu, Rumpa Behen(because I promised you once that I'll mention about you in my first book), My Abin Pai, Akang Dada, Ammi, Ania moi and Kai Mama.

Thank You all for existing!

Prologue

I give to you,
A part of me,
That was never unveiled.
I give to you,
All of me,
In every word,
That's been said;
In each turn of the page.
Word by word,
I tell you, all my tale.
I mend my words,
And write to you,
A tragedy of mine.
Cause I give to you a part of me,
Well, all of me, I guess.
@charumoni

1. The water-colour

• 1 •

Like the light stains on a fragile sheet,
Of a Periwinkle dream.
Our Youth is saved,
In matters of Memories and Moments.
Flickering like the citylights,
Away in the country sky.
Like the greys of a rainy Mondays,
Or the blues of a Sunny Wednesday sky.
Our Youth is like the Stains,
Of the water colours;
Soft, light and fragile,
Still the tint that never lets go.
Just like how the stains of the water colour stays,
The script of our youth stays forever in our hearts,
A story on repeat,
Just like the fragile dye of the water-colour.

2. Ever Be

I do not remember the last time,

You crossed my mind.

Cause you're in all the,

Red and cream combination.

In all the places,

We used to cross paths.

You linger in all the tall shadows,

I cannot see through.

You are so alive in my memories,

To ever fade in my reality.

And you are everywhere I am,

And you are everywhere I'll ever be.

3. The wild Rose

March is here,
And all the pretty flowers,
Will spring and bloom.
To where the road is,
And almost everywhere around.
Pretty in all shades and shapes.
But the wild rose,
White and almost everywhere,
Is not pretty enough,
To get noticed.
It is almost everywhere,
All time of the year to care.
But, sometimes that wild rose,
Needs a little love,
A little appreciation,
Not for the beauty,
But simply for existing.
Cause the wild rose decorates all the paths.
That Wild Rose is me,
That Wild Rose is you,
That Wild Rose is us,
Somewhere in the crowd.
Existing quietly, among the seasonal,

Showers of our life.

4. That White

The Colour white represents,
My existence in disguise.
Not because I'm pure,
Or I symbolise peace.
But because, it's afraid.
Of getting replaced with other colours,
Overpowering her own identity.
I am that white,
That gets easily stained on;
With colours as light as blue or pink.
I am that White in disguise.
The walls of my heart is,
White-washed in bright white.
Not because it's well lighted,
Or perfectly stable inside.
But because this heart is scared,
Of getting attacked with fresh,
Wounds of scars and bruishes,
Of being brushed in some other paints,
Overpowering the white in me,
This white is afraid, of not being the vision,
I paint for myself. That White!

5. The Alley

The Alley next to my window,
Holds in it, a memory,
Flickering away from my album,
Of a happy dream.
The alley near the brick wall,
Decorated in orange trumpet vines,
Or the white Bougainvillea,
During a Rainy summer noon.
The Alley stays next to my heart,
Standing the test of time.
Holding on a memory,
Glimmering away in ashes of the happy dreams.

6. Time and Places

He smelt like the rural Earth,

And felt like the morning dew of a summer morn.

He smiles in a distant land,

Away from the crowded streets,

Away from my time.

He lay under the stars' light,

And I wandered in a lonely citylight.

He is covered under the shades,

Of roses and lavenders;

Wild, yet so pretty.

We were meant to be,

Or we were just not.

Cause you are further than,

The Forever I ever knew,

And the Forever I'll ever know.

7. An Old Story

From the recollection of a past treasure,
An old story,
Buried 'neath the paper bags,
In a rusted casket of bygone disc.
Knocked over the Greyish Floor.
Waking up all the dormant memories,
Of that summer Noon.
A time in my life,
When all the birds were a waking call,
And the smell of the books,
Were a morning delight.
A time when my life was like a dream,
In an open sky,
Like a yellow kite:
Over the green fields of a July Sky.
A time in my life when,
All that glitters was indeed gold.
All the days, a caramel dream,
And felt like a tropical berry.
That brought back all the memories,
A memory from my old story.

8. Respiration

• 9 •

We are like the process of Respiration,
Weaved together in a single breath.
The only diference is,
I "inhale" to let you in,
And you "exhale" to let me go.

9. Home

My space,
Is not white enough,
Not pretty enough,
And not aesthetic enough,
For the settings to shine on,
The trending cassestte roll.
My space has horrible,
Ivy outgrowns,
Pieces of the old newspapers,
Spread across the uneven lane,
Of the overgrown garden area.
My space has creeking doors,
Rusting irons of the open verandah.
Broken glasses,
Uneven shattered tiles,
And a story that didn't end well.
My space is without a safe shelter,
To smile through the day.
My space is scattered in,
Fights and torn,
Into the yellings across the room.
That is how flawed my space is.
Scars, curses and grey walls.

Flooding album of tears;
And a happy memory,
That could not stood the test of the time.
Still,
My Space is all for me,
My Space is all of me.
My space is where I breathe in the freedom.
My space is where I am at peace.
This space is my Home,
Where every piece of my childhood,
Was spent in catching dragonflies,
Picking wild flowers and lantana berries,
And watching the blue sky.
This space is my Home,
Which mends and herbals my broken soul,
Screens through my school days,
And album my thoughts.
This space is my favourite place,
In this whole wide world.
This place is my only Home,
In all the greys of the life.

10. Head and Heart

A blue wednesday shined with scattered stars,
Yellow sunset and Vanilla Twilight.
Branches branched the dark edges of my saddened spine.
A conflict notes the tale of a head and a heart.
The drowning heart and barren head travelled dispersely
away,
Love, life and desire cemented on the dusty path.
The boiling knocks of life, troubles the child inside,
This war narrates the tale of the head and the heart.
The space bridges the chorus of the head,
And the heart burden herself with dateless ring of misery.
The head streches all the corners of the Earthy Flesh,
And the heart hurts everytime the band hits the soul.
The notes are written for the voices,
The head and heart narrates.
Over the water that washed over you.

11. The Last Lullaby

Sing to me a lullaby,
So that I can close my eyes.
To hear our song before I die,
And bade to you one last goodbye.
Sing to me a lullaby,
So that I can re-live my life.
A life, that just passed by,
And sleep forever without a sigh.
Sing to me one last tribute,
So as to hear you in, for the last minute.
So as to live even when I'll fade,
In all the memories that we made.

12. Falling Season

Early Maturity is like,
The season of fall.
Things withers,
The Green rusts,
There are no pretty flowers,
And air turns decidious.
Its suicide.
However,
It is like an early lesson,
For all the things that is yet to come.
It is a shelter,
For the looming heartaches.
Like a summer sweater,
For the approaching winter.
Meant to save us,
From all the worst,
That is yet to come.

13. Stories

Some stories are just stories,

Not Love Stories.

And ours, we fall in that very ordinary stories.

We are just stories,

Meant to play the part,

In the scene,

And dissappear,

In a blink.

14. Ordinary People

We're just ordinary people.
A little simple,
A little too complicated.
A soul in love,
A soul wanting to be loved.
We're just ordinary people.
A little scared,
A little too early matured.
A soul that gets easily anxious,
A soul needing an another soul to rely on.
And we are just ordinary people.
A little tired,
A little too sad.
So, can we be a little too Humane too?
Cause we're just ordinary people anyway.

15. The Marigold Tree

With this tiny young hands,

I spread the seed,

Of an old Marigold harvest.

For weeks and so on,

I watered it right,

And kept it under my young, bright eyes.

It grew with love,

Into this big, bushy green

Into a Marigold Tree.

Taller than me,

In just Weeks time.

With it's soft green stems,

Branching the corners,

Of my Marigold heaven.

I watched in awe,

And so mesmerized.

At the sight of the orange Marigold light.

That the Four year old,

Nurtured and mothered.

Such was the joy,

I had in me,

Such was the pride I carried within.

I watched it grow into,

These tall Marigold tree,
That was once just a seed.
This was such much more for me,
To turn;
The old harvest,
Into the flowery tree.

16. The Lighthouse

Covered in Concrete and dead grass,
Dressed warmly like the season of fall;
Slightly orange and little yellow,
In between the sun and the frost;
Be my lighthouse a place I can go.
Whenever the tsunami in me,
Rises upto the core.
Be my Lighthouse,
A little patient,
A little kind.
You smell like the summer rose,
And taste like the winter coffee,
Slightly mild on all the sides,
In between the sweet and sour;
Be my lighthouse,
Concrete and strong.
So that we can star gaze,
And see through the storms,
Hand and hand, together.
In love and friendship.

17. From Afar

I'll still love you from afar,
And I'll still love you from a distance,
For my love is too much,
To expect even a bit of it.
My love is in the will to wait for hours,
And in the spaces between the books in the library,
In the window pane,
You stood a minute or so,
And in the freshly sketched ink you signed on.
And I'll still love you from afar,
And I'll still love you from a distance,
For I know that,
I can only love you in the poems I write to you,
And the verses I spell on the pages.
So, even when you're times away,
Even when I can't have you in my days,
Allow me to have you in my nights,
In my dreams and in my thoughts,
Forever in my memories.

18. I wish Upon this Thistle

From the garden of long dreams,
And lifelong wishes,
I plucked it off,
The thistle, a wishing belief.
One, out of the thousands,
I threaded my hopes into it.
The light fell under the wide blue sky.
I aired a deep breath and Lo!
It fluff and flipped away.
To travel far and beyond;
Away in a land unknown.
It swept past the winds of change,
And walked on forever by,
It walked away with my wishes,
Like it has to fill the Vow.
Naked and alone,
It stayed so proud,
With a pact to sign.
A thistle to wish upon.
For better or for worse.
And I wish upon this thistle to keep you safe,
I wish upon this thistle to home you a bed,

I wish upon this thistle to bring you back,

Not to me,

But to the God,

Who never gave up on you.

19. In the Mist

With the Mountains towering the sky,
My imagination outstriped the level of limit.
It chimed the verses I had on my mind.
And eventually sketched the paper with ink.
The time elapsed and the mist loomed in,
Leisurely and gloomy it seemed to me.
Rhyming a lullaby, sheathing the hills,
Carolling it in depth; hallucinating the wind, the field.
Although, the Mist sketched the setting in white,
The Mountains lived in the mist without a fight.
So, I treasured this transient sight on my mind,
And spelled life to this tale, with verses played in rhymes.

20. I'll Find You

• 24 •

In this piece of thin sheet,
In this body of paper soul,
I'll carve a map of the road,
That leads to you.
In this old typewriter,
I've wrote verses and verses,
All onto your way,
Towards your heart.
Though you are still times away,
Away in the impending days.
And I can't figure you out right away,
I'll find you anyway.
I promise this to you,
I will find you.

21. The Verses

• 25 •

And I shall perish oneday,

Into the soil,

Like a name never known,

A life, never lived.

However,

I will still be living in my verses,

Which will plant her seeds,

In every words,

Every new rhymes,

That will escape your lips.

In all the voices that will read me through,

And I will live in them,

Somehow,

For ever and always.

22. The Distance

To the gaps that I failed to fill,
To the miles, I couldn't measure,
To the distance that travelled,
In parallel lines.
I hope to walk with you oneday.
There was just a centimetre between us,
But that made all the difference.
Like the border of all the seasons,
Yours spring, While I fall.
You see the summer sun,
While I grow cold.
To the distance that displaced our hearts,
To the miles that created the snows,
I once hope to walk with you,
And I still long to walk with you.
Walking this distance for you,
With you.

23. A Shadow

Like a shadow on a black night,
I was always there.
In a dimmed light,
Next to your side.
I lived like a blurred print,
Of an old damaged photograph.
I was always halved in a corner of your smile.
A stranger of the crowd.
Longing for a homely welcome,
And warm side of you,
I become a shadow to even my own self,
And in lives of all the people I've known.
Like a shadow,
I'll always be unknown.
Cause a Shadow is,
Always dark and unnoticed.

24. Black Night

Far away,
In Mid-Pacific,
On the mid summer of,
Highly pitched night,
I trouble my heart again.
My heart wondered,
Away in the woods,
Of a country farm.
In the old bridge of my town,
Sweet, yet sad.
In between these thought,
A yellow sun shined.
I dreamed a minute longer.
It troubled my mind,
It ache and drenched through my bones.
Far away,
In Mid-Atlantic,
I wrote a verse for my home,
A green colour of the walls,
Smelled sweet to my hurting soul.
Should I walk back?
Or let the sea sail me through,
The unknown world,

For the waves to decide,
I do not know.
I took an aging sheet,
And painted a map.
A map, that looked like my home,
A map that I left somewhere,
I cannot find.
Should I follow the prints I left behind?
Or let it get rained on?
To move on ahead.
Should I borrow an Umbrella?
Or the rain is the remedy to my tragedy,
I cannot decide.
Far away,
In mid-pacific,
I miss my home.
While I lay in my bed alone.

25. The Comforting Tree

I left my home,
And travelled through the forest road.
Away into an unknown town,
To read through my youth.
Away from my home. In wilderness.
But out into this foreign town,
Felt so jittery to me.
I wished I can just walk back home
Cause I feared of all the odds,
That was yet to come.
I wandered alone,
To where the road ends,
And came across this big yellow tree.
A wooden gate stood underneath'
This Giant tree flowered in yellow leaves.
As I stood watching the decaying gate in awe,
Deep in my thoughtful world.
The yellow leaves showered;
All its flowering leaves upon me,
Melting all my fears away.
This tree comforted my soul,
Whenever I was stressed.
It mended my weakening spirit,

By flowering in Pink,
Yellow and green.
This is an ode to my comforting tree,
That stood tall and strong,
Showering everytime I stood underneath'
The tree that always fall upon,
A complete stranger like me.

"There is a magic tree in Midland, Roing which was my comfort space. And standing under the tree was always a blessing for me. It always showered upon me, its flowers or leaves whenever I stood underneath. And it felt like magic to me. So, I wrote an ode to you so as to let you know that I was at a safe haven because of your existence.

"

26. A Memory

Walking through the same old road,
Reminded me of you.
Like it was just yesterday,
We were careless, wild and free.
The long road through,
The summer sunset,
Of wild growing pampas,
And sound of the flowing water.
A perfect scene,
Right from the movie screen.
It felt like just yesterday,
When we talked about us,
And I said it was just a phase and not really love,
You frown and disagreed with me.
I laugh out loud,
And bet it on with you.
Now as I walk through the same old road,
And you are not with me,
I said to myself, that I was right.
It really was never meant to be.

27. Yellow Paper

From the yellow sheet,
Of coloured paper.
I wrote to me,
A happy Poem.
A happy rhyme,
Of nursery songs.
Of the tender growth,
And a loving home.
From the yellow sheet,
Of coloured paper,
I wrote to me,
A happy dream,
A dream where I was young,
Where nothing was ever wrong,
Just swinging down the sycamore tree,
Without a care of the adult world.
Now, on the same sheet of yellow paper,
I write myself to sleep.
Some songs are sad,
Some rather depressed,
No happy poems to show.
What went so wrong,
While growing up.

I guess I'll never know.

28. Forever

Forever is a long time.
Older than the forever,
Ever known,
A Forever larger than,
Infinity and beyond.
Longer than the Forever,
Ever expressed.
And a Forever,
Ever kept.
Forever is a myth.

29. An Episode

As you lay in your last bed,
Without a voice,
Without a sound.
I watch your eyes,
And rewind the old times,
In the last 7 minutes,
Of your life.
We grew in the outskirts,
Away from the city roads.
Into a paradise,
Of wild flowers and berries.
Into the country sky,
Where the stars garnish the night.
As you lay cold in your wooden cist,
And I play your favourite ballad,
You do not break into a smile,
Like you used to.
And my belief that you would,
Is shattered into sands.
It's been years since,
I last saw you.
But I dreamt about you today,
And I guess I'll never wake again,

Cause my bed smell of the daffodils,
Of your cemetery bed.

• 37 •

30. Someone Like you

Whenever I close my eyes,
And ponder about the time I'd die,
I will miss all the times we had,
The moments that were always great.
You stands like a piece of art,
That has stood strong in my heart.
You are like a light to my darkness,
A song to my happiness.
When I'll be faded and gone,
I won't ever want to see you alone,
Shedding all the adored tears,
In days that'll turn to years.
I am always there in your memories,
And all the soulful lullabies,
Always remember I am with you,
Cause I will forever be happy that I met someone like you.

31. The Mountains

I know I'm not pretty,
And I might not posses the thing of beauty,
But I won't let it derive me away from my duty,
Because I know what are my responsibilities.
I have to scale thousands of mountains,
And Combat back my pain,
A million list of lessons to gain,
Before I sleep forever in this land.
I have to step forward to face the world,
To turn the coal to pearl,
To fight more battles for being a girl,
But I won't let it ruin my will.
I might grey and fade oneday,
But won't let it ravage my day.
Cause I know it's not today,
And it might takes years to hit me one day.

32. Just A Passer By

I am not the lead,
The light do not fall on me,
When the shoot begins.
I am just a character,
Behind the scenes,
In the bad cuts.
Sometimes blurred,
To enhance the beauty of the lead.
I hope I don't let myself,
Forever play this part;
Atleast in my own story,
I deserve to be the lead.
A story that actually revolves around me.
Not a sideline,
But an actual character of,
My ordinary life.

33. The Marigolds

To the Marigolds,
My favourite sight.
I owe to you,
My heart and my soul.
You hold in me a comfort space.
Of your melancholic embrace.
To the Marigolds,
My secret love affair.
My heart melts in your air,
And dear Darlin, I'm sure you're aware.
Of all the flaws I own:
The fear of being disowned.
To the Marigolds,
In a field far away,
In a scented country cottage,
Of a distant village.
Shower all your comfort,
Out into the world.
For the World still don't know you yet,
Like the way I do since forever and more.

34. Somewhere, Somehow

Somewhere, somehow,
Oneday.
Under a gloomy,
Moonsoon sky.
In a Summerly decorated,
Night sky.
Or in a windy,
Autmn evening.
We will meet again.
Somewhere, somehow,
Someday,
Under the cherry tree,
Covered in sweet blow,
On the snow covered bridge,
Of olden times,
Or in the outskirt valley,
Of Marigold showers.
We will meet again.
Under the same sky,
That on looked our farewell.
The same road that divided us,
Will connect our track.
We will rewrite this story

With the bookay of cosmos,
That starred in the dawn.
And, somehow
We will meet again.

35. The Breath

I breathe it in,
I breathe it out.
It comes so naturally,
Without much trys'.
It's thrust lived in shade,
Till I could breathe no more.
Like a corpse,
I decayed for days.
And when it ended,
It was already a week.
Flipping in all sides,
Through the thinniest shade.
I let it in,
I let it out.
All the air so naturally.
It came like it was never there.
It's gist lived in dark,
Till I could breathe no more.

"*P.S : I wrote it when I recovered from a week long fight with the trouble of breathing. I hope many can relate.*"

36. Maybe

And maybe I,
Didn't know what he,
Was going through.
And maybe He,
Had no idea about,
The pains and sufferings,
On my side of the field.
Maybe We both,
Had no roles to play,
In this tragic opera.
But Maybe,
We were suppose cross paths,
In one scene of the play.
Meant to hurt each other,
To the core of the Cancer.
Ending each other to the ashes,
Of what what life could hold;
Only for us.

37. Other side of Grey

I see the waves;
Huge grey waves of clouds.
It's depressing and death like.
I see the rainbows,
It's brightness disgusts me,
It smells like a goodbye from the other side.
I see flowers,
I love the bloom,
And it scares me a little too.
Am I strange?
I try to build relationships,
But I end up cutting everyone,
Out of my world.
I do not know how to love people,
So, I give away the love they send my way,
Since I give a little,
I do not deserve a lot.
So, I birch myself,
And make everybody leave.
Because no one deserves to know my heart.
It's dark and cruel in there.

38. Like A Pressed Flower

I keep you like the pressed flower,
In between the stages of my life.
In the days that left,
And days that are still yet to come.
Wrinkled in ageing,
And longevity,
Of an old track,
Of my favourite song.
I keep you like a presesed flower,
In hopes of a light string,
Of love; Amor Fati.
Or the red thread of fate,
Even if it is decaying.
Even in fading memories.
Somewhere safe,
Somewhere in me.
I keep you like a pressed flower,
In an old, beautiful memory.
Of my youthful days.
In between love and hatred,
Forever growing with me.
In the wild moors,
And daisy days;

Of my Amnesiac dreams.
And you live like a pressed flower,
Deep within my grey heart,
Like an old scar.
A treasured relic of my love.
Forever and always,
Buried in me,
Living in me.

39. Sky Full of Stars

The sky went darkish tonight,

And the insides of mine,

Went messed up as it forever was.

But the night flickered,

And Boom! The sky got decoarated,

With the lamps of the stars.

I ran out in the freezing cold.

As I saw the light,

In the midst of the hopelessness.

You stared in the sky above,

And I was hopeless no more.

I saw words,

In the constellation,

And placed them,

On the table of my blank sheet.

The Stars above,

Gleam in the darkness,

Of the solitary night.

Singing a song for the,

Hopeful days to come.

Cause when I am confined in,

Between darkness and without the light,

There is more room for,

The brightness to shine.

40. Forgive me once, Forgive me not

The Air smells of Spring,

And the Sorrow of the Fall is,

In the process of healing.

I once had a happy dream,

A happily ever after.

The flowers have bloom,

At a distant, at noon;

Creeping in, I found a shelter.

A house, not a home.

The Pillow is coarse and heavy,

It hurts my neck, but it is always okay,

For the heart has suffered since cradle,

I know how to put on an act and suffer alone.

"Forgive me once,

Forgive me not.

But let me forgive myself.
"

I watch my line,

Whenever I share some smiles.

I fake my joy,

To heal the crowd:

What could not heal in me.

I cut my veins,

The arteries ruptures,

It bleeds in sweats,

That cannot be seen.

I see my bones, the cuts, the scars.

To hide it all,

I pretend a little,

A day, a month then a decade mirrors my heart.

"*Forgive me once,*

Forgive me not.

But can I please forgive myself for once?
"

41. A Sweet Dream

Unaware of the bustling crowd,
I drifted away into the clouds,
Floating between the white and Blues,
Of an unknown dream.
I waved at every single things I saw;
To the waves
The planes,
The boats,
And the submarines.
Unaware of the settling crowd,
And the wavering sounds.
I look back and saw the paths,
Paved with rainbow bricks,
And gleaming ivy.
Right beneath the grey Mural.
It calmed my mind,
And gripped my heart,
Like a song,
That only I can relate.

42. An Apology

While dusting the old notes,

An old photograph slipped,

Under my creeky bed.

I crawled and reached out and saw,

The smile that once lit my face,

The smile I lost on the way,

To where the present is now screened.

The times we had was,

A long time ago,

And a bygone era,

I did not care to touch again.

But the old snapshot brought to life,

The times I spent with you.

We looked the happiest,

The happiest I can ever be.

Without a care,

Of times ahead.

My heart drummed a beat we used to hum,

And played the lyrics within my mind,

I wished to run back in time.

The old image was fading from the corners,

The damage done by the sea water,

I guess I can write to you,

That I am as sorry as I can ever be.
So, this is an apology to who it is meant for,
I guess you guessed it right,
This is for all the hearts,
That once loved me.

43. Evergreen Tree

You existed like the,
White wildflowers in the walkways,
Smiling throughout the drought,
And heavy Monsoon.
You existed like the,
Green wild grass in the way back to my home,
Getting stepped on,
But never missed to smile.
You existed like the,
Usual Sparrows in the sky above,
It never excites the crowd beneath.
Your existence never mattered much.
But to me,
You are an evergreen tree,
No matter where I stand,
You would always spring and green.
And it mattered more than,
Seasonal flowers to me.
Cause you hold the ground with me,
Whether it winters or fall in me.
You are like a perfect forever,
That will forever mean so much more to me.

44. The Poisoned Living

Decendants of this earth started with slavery,
Chained, caged and sold at large.
A love story that could never begin,
And a future that never rhymed with notes.
The century crippled the people in debt and agony,
No dreams ever dreamed,
And the dream that never led to a miracle.
The land onced called the Gem of Earth,
Positioned itself with quakes,
Travelling parallel with destruction.
Freedom came with tragic eyes,
Scattered light, no future to passage the next day.
The water swallowed the field,
The life, the Haiti destroyed.
People baked iron-hard bread to survive,
A bread made up of soil.
Soaked in sun and flavoured by salt,
A means of survival,
But a poisoned living.

45. Water Underneath'

The water from the canal,
Is underneath my feet.
They rise at levels, with waves,
Throwing petty tantrums.
The plants I digged in soil,
Is flooded. The roots are up,
And too much of everything,
Kills it all. All of it.
My bones smells like rusted irons,
Exposed to crowd, overthinking and self doubt.
A never ending chain of sorrows,
Unwritten in blank pages,
Visibly dark. Drunk in confusion,
Yet the path is very long and weary.
There's just water underneath,
Rusted seeds of a funeral song.
Tuned in with grey skies,
Dark clouds and long, lonely nights.

46. The Peach Tree

With the winter winds gushing through,
The Open window.
Caressing my skin and my soul,
Shifting my mood,
Into the sight of the wild grass,
And in the carols of the summer flowers.
As I sit by the window,
And watch the fading peach flowers,
My heart printed a sweet lullaby,
Of the summer folksongs,
Fruiting the flowers of the peach tree,
Represents more than just the look.
Illustrating that the fading youth,
Of the beautiful days,
Brings with it, the hope for
The days ahead filled with,
Experience, knowledge and wisdom,
That can last a lifetime.

47. The Ending

There was so much in the air,
The day you left our home,
It was never home again,
Just a building with some memories.
There was so much weight in our hearts,
The day you decided to abandone us,
We could never love again,
Cause our only love left us for another love.
There was so much questions we had in us,
The day you said it was easier to live without us,
Cause all our life,
We were tryin our best to stay with you.
There was so much hatred in us,
Not for you, but ourselves.
Because maybe we made you left,
Or maybe we were just never enough.
But the day you left,
Every single emotion we hold,
Left with you. We could trust no more,
And love no more.
Cause a new love grew within your heart,
That made our love less for you.
And if the only love,

That was once so sacred,
Could hurt people to doubt their existence,
I doubt the very idea of love,
Much more than I ever did.
Much more than I ever will.